Marc Vincenz

# The Visitation

*A Fishy Novelette in Reverse*

**SurVision Books**

First published in 2024 by
SurVision Books
Dublin, Ireland
Reggio di Calabria, Italy
www.survisionmagazine.com


Copyright © Marc Vincenz, 2024

Cover image: © Sophia Santos, 2024


ISBN: 978-1-912963-48-5


This book is in copyright. No part of this publication may be reproduced, stored in a retrieval system, or transmitted in any form or by any means without the prior permission in writing from the publisher.

## Notes and Acknowledgments

The quotation, "... *small, distant world, a token of our sounds, our science, our images, our music, our thoughts and our feelings*," in "Chapter Four: *The Golden Anchovy Grooves*," was something President Jimmy Carter said, when the *Voyager* Golden Record, a 12-inch gold-plated copper disk containing sounds and images selected to portray the diversity of life and culture on Earth, was inserted into her very own space vessel.

The lines "The only way to cool it is with baboon's blood," and "The charm is firm and good," in "Chapter Eight: *Every Seventh Creature*," both hail from Billy Shankspur's *Macbeth*.

CONTENTS

| | |
|---|---|
| CHAPTER ONE: *Crab God of Sand, Ocean, and Sky* | 5 |
| CHAPTER TWO: *She Who Claims to Be a Prophet* | 10 |
| CHAPTER THREE: *They Who Changed Their Minds* | 12 |
| CHAPTER FOUR: *The Golden Anchovy Grooves* | 15 |
| CHAPTER FIVE: *Where the Myth Begins* | 18 |
| CHAPTER SIX: *A Sun in Any Other Galaxy* | 21 |
| CHAPTER SEVEN: *Every Seventh Creature* | 27 |
| CHAPTER EIGHT:<br>*In This Strange Fashion the Twins Were Reborn* | 30 |
| CHAPTER NINE: *Watershed Moment* | 33 |
| EPILOGUE: *Still in the Dark* | 38 |

**Chapter One**

*Crab God of Sand, Ocean, and Sky*

In a dark seething fury, the god wades through
their oceanic green, through churning shale and froth

where minnows swirl around their spiny legs
and piperfish nip at their eyestalks. Yes, they know how

to calm their seas, to tend the waves and maelstroms,
to direct the leaping of the faithful flying fish;

and it goes without saying, to grasp the undying
love tentacles of the Great Cosmic Squid ...

Beneath the giant Ferris wheel burdened with the bounties
of limitless two-legged landlocked sand-gazing voyagers,

a rattling tumor coughs thick dark fumes on the beach;
and, from its grim posterior, long black tentacles of disgrace

splash through the shallows until they melt into the foam.
Seagulls and tuna are caught in a frenzy of tar

and feather and pitch, herring whip to the surface;
fully clawed, the kittiwake screams

and swoops in.

And the blackened shrimp
rise and fall in a strange

dark, undulating spume;
the ocean here smells primordial,

as if she is escaping to her erstwhile
self; the crab god swallows

mouthfuls of water and brine,
waves retreat all along the shore ...

and then, and there is a pause
of limitless silence,

a pause so long
it seems time

herself has ended.
Before the storm,

the sand turns to clear glass;
after the storm, there is nothing

but fragments and fleas.

## Chapter Two

*She Who Claims to Be a Prophet*


Down at the pier, across from the arcade hall,
the seer makes herself known in all her dark colors,

the shift of the lace against her thin skin; even the squeak
of her shoe soles has a gruff reprimanding growl.

Some days known as Madame Mardi Gras, others
as Mrs. Flash-in-the-Pan; and by word, the sparks

she could set alight: the Whirlygigs and Spinning Jennys,
little flashes of insight into the un-jimmied mind.

"There is nothing before the storm," she says gazing
into a teacup, "but I see here something after."

Her eyes twinkle; the hands flatten the tablecloth,
then she reaches for your fingers, straightens them

into the flat palm of her mind; behind, the curtain
rustles, a cool breeze teases the knees, the toes tingle.

"Tonight all things come to an end," she says,
then drains her cup until the very last drop.

## Chapter Three

*They Who Changed Their Minds*

Several years earlier, when Madeline sat on the Council, the local district ratified the vote. Madeline, like most,

was a 'yea;' Theo, of course, was a 'nay.' His father sat fretfully in on the City's cocktail party, mine heavily

on the Zoning Commission. And bored he was. Boring into himself with his quick fixes and those mini red pills

of hydromoxiboralide; guaranteed to keep you calm in the most crucial moments, said the doc.

My father swore by them in his darkest hours, or so
goes the lore; then, here goes the neighborhood.

*Toot! Toot!* went the rooster like a passing train—at least
ours did when he was pecking for this season's mate.

Father, perched on the porch railings, sniffing our own
musty glue, was contemplating the rate of exchange.

Information was to be had in those circular fliers
the Church plastered the walls and ceilings with.

"More information than you'd likely need," said Mother, stirring the herbaceous family casserole with her wooden spoon;

still, the cat ran up the clock, and it chimed well before the vote. The Planning Commission was meeting with the Zoning Board.

They hired Fanny's Fish & Chips to cater the affair, and apparently, Theo's father brought along his chained bear,

Kumquat, who danced and roared to the minor gods of sand and sea, and they answered him in kind, or so goes the lore.

**Chapter Four**

*The Golden Anchovy Grooves*

Once this fishing town was rife with their shoals;
a mating ground for humpbacks and their royal moray foray,

piperfish grazed the sandbanks like angry wisps of the deep;
and the anchovy spawning and dying in all their glories.

Hardly a bucket or a pail was left empty. You could scoop
your hand into the ocean, and there was your live catch;

dozens of them wriggling in your palm. They were salted
and oiled, dried and smoked; some marinated in tomato

and garlic were to be the main course for the annual raffle
of the Garundia Tabernacle Choir; and after the feast,

the bones were discarded all along the shores, as evidence
for the majestic gestures of the evening before; but when Tomas

spat out the bones, he discovered something entirely un-
expected, namely, a little plastic nametag with his name

engraved in it in a somewhat juvenile script; on the back,
a missive—his friends took it as something of a fortune cookie—

(I imagined it more like the *Voyager* Golden Record, a grooved time capsule sent off into the deep from this *small, distant world,*

*a token of our sounds, our science, our images, our music, our thoughts and our [innermost] feelings.*

The inner eye from way over there.) It said:

*Although we die at your hands, we live forever in your reef.*

And then, it said: *How do you think you'll swim out of this?*

Before he died, the Golden Anchovy approached Tomas
in a dream and guided his salty soul straight into the deep.

**Chapter Five**

*Where the Myth Begins*

The Visitors descend from out of these spheres
simply as an afterthought, a droplet of cosmic intention—

this all occurs sometime in the waking hours
between five-thirty and six—Madeline knows this,

for in these hours her sick child, like a rooster,
caws into the dawn, yearning to bask in the early rays

of violet and indigo and blush; this seems to attract them.
They move strangely, in a motion never witnessed before.

If one were to try to decode it into a *lingua franca*,
it might be like silkworm threads meeting a gentle trickle

of aquifer; *only, there is something cold about them,
and not just to the touch.* "Life lives within a bottle," they say,

tugging their ears, and then, "We are that empty bottle,"
they retort; they swear to free her from her yokes she calls

fashion statements. Clasping the symbol to her bosom,
she says, "I know this: the mythology survives. It lives

in the faces of carved stone that gaze down from the past."
For an instant, the Visitors survey the diminishing horizon,

then in close-encounter-kind, say, "Eventually everything will crumble to dust or coal or sand or be squashed into sticky oils."

## Chapter Six

*A Sun in Any Other Galaxy*

Part One:
*It's hard to explain where this all began.*

Was it
in the sub-
conscious
uncon-
scious
or the con-
scious sub-
conscious,
my love?

Was it
in the word
or in the line,
in the heft
of the chisel
on marble or
maybe just
the tone herself:
the singsong, which
was but a mimicry
(some would say,
a mockery or malarkey)
of the language
of avatars and aviators?

Was it
in the haphazard-
at-the-surface, yet
fractal and, Fibonacci-
esque beneath?

She always thought so.

(A theorem like this that defies the known laws of the quantum, but still works, possibly?)

Part Two:
*The Soul Seekers*

Was it
in the prob-
lems of the sliding-
scale of the mela-
tonin in our skins?
The color of
our scales,
the sparkles in
our eyes?

(Or was it just in the eternal churning of milky rivers?)

All I can say is, that night, every creature raised their heads, pricked up their ears and receivers, and sat or hovered or swayed silently in great anticipation.

*Life must be renewed*, they called out.

*Blood must be born from within*, they sang and croaked and howled and bellowed and guffawed and clucked and bleated and buzzed and …

In the end, when all the rare metals converged, it had to taste right.

## Chapter Seven

*Every Seventh Creature*

*One doctor to another:*

"He has a dominant gene, and thus, as their forefathers predicted, the more useful traits hang on, amplified, intensified."

*Another doctor to one:*

"Perhaps this, then, the reason for all these bizarre afflictions among the crossbred youth of today."

*A third doctor pitches in:*

"There was an era where this was all discovered: among the first bankers in the world rose the first artists and scientists and barber-surgeons."

"And don't forget the witches," says One.

"The only way to cool it is with baboon's blood," says Another.

"Let the lightning strike," says a Third.

Their charm is firm and good.

## Chapter Eight

*In This Strange Fashion the Twins Were Reborn*

Part One:

And thrived, but in their shrieking, the words intensified, never mind the rapture, never mind that wished-for element of surprise.

"But, as we all know, hay is never sown before the dawn," she thought, stroking her feathers. "And wheat, ne'er harvested before the sunrise," thought her twin sister scraping the earth.

They had spent the morning strutting at the edges of the woods, peeking and pecking for those juicy wood bugs. They swore to each other they should never be apart their entire lives; and they groomed and plumed each other every night as they settled into their mossy caves and contemplated their mossy future and who lay in it.

Part Two:

In their dreams there came this rooster so pleasantly attired in the quills of emperors: each of their multifarious colors, a hint at what he had been up to heretofore: red was war, orange was for abundant apricot trees, blue was for clear skies and dewdrops, and green, green was for the inside—and darker still—how far.

In his dawning songs, he promised each of them the ends of the earth and more. It was so easy to believe him in the twilight.

He promised them mayflies and jumping spiders, crisp little acorn-sized weevils; he promised he would take care of his twin-sister wives, and would give them rain and abundant sunshine, and as many offspring as Krookroo, the rooster god, would ask for.

Part Three:

And so, in their dream, the twin sisters considered their options, consulted the oracle and the fates, tossed the bones of their ur-ancestors.

*The credits were rolling, but they had made up their minds.*

All told and forsworn, they forgot about the sunrise.

## Chapter Nine

*Watershed Moment*

Every once in a while she flickers, or rather the space where she later appears flickers—it's as if she's being brought in from another version of this other planet in the habitable zone.

Madeline is five and picking wildflowers.

Bees and damselflies crisscross the pasture in an elegant show of pollination and honey; spiders weave stalks together with their threads; silkworms dangle in the trees and somewhere, far up on the edge of the woods, there's movement in the tall grass.

She clasps a purple looking-glass and a speckled touch-me-not; she doesn't pull them, though. She strokes their petals and plays with a tiny green caterpillar.

She can hear the roar of a blustery ocean, but here in the pasture life ambles serenely on, content with a single sun's solar radiation and all her clouds welling and shifting, headed to the coast.

Above a mollusk shell slowly shifts over the sky, blocking out the sun, moon and stars.

Everything goes dark.

**Epilogue**

*Still in the Dark*

In the dark, clasping her flowers, Madeline says:

Where are you, God?

As far as she can tell, there's no answer.

# Selected Poetry Titles Published by SurVision Books

**Contemporary Tangential Surrealist Poetry: An Anthology**
Edited by Tony Kitt
ISBN 978-1-912963-44-7

**Seeds of Gravity: An Anthology of Contemporary Surrealist Poetry from Ireland**
Edited by Anatoly Kudryavitsky
ISBN 978-1-912963-18-8

**Invasion: An Anthology of Ukrainian Poetry about the War**
Edited by Tony Kitt
ISBN 978-1-912963-32-4

**Noelle Kocot.** *Humanity*
(New Poetics: USA)
ISBN 978-1-9995903-0-7

**Marc Vincenz.** *Einstein Fledermaus*
(New Poetics: USA)
ISBN 978-1-912963-20-1

**Helen Ivory.** *Maps of the Abandoned City*
(New Poetics: England)
ISBN 978-1-912963-04-1

**Tony Kitt.** *The Magic Phlute*
(New Poetics: Ireland)
ISBN 978-1-912963-08-9

**John W. Sexton.** *Inverted Night*
(New Poetics: Ireland)
ISBN 978-1-912963-05-8

**Clayre Benzadón.** *Liminal Zenith*
(New Poetics: USA)
ISBN 978-1-912963-11-9

**Thomas Townsley.** *Tangent of Ardency*
(New Poetics: USA)
ISBN 978-1-912963-15-7

**Mikko Harvey & Jake Bauer.** *Idaho Falls*
(Winner of James Tate Poetry Prize 2018)
ISBN 978-1-912963-02-7

**John Bradley.** *Spontaneous Mummification*
(Winner of James Tate Poetry Prize 2019)
ISBN 978-1-912963-13-3

**John Thomas Allen.** *Rolling in the Third Eye*
(Winner of James Tate Poetry Prize 2019)
ISBN 978-1-912963-15-7

**Charles Kell.** *Pierre Mask*
(Winner of James Tate Poetry Prize 2019)
ISBN 978-1-912963-19-5

**Jon Riccio.** *Eye, Romanov*
(Winner of James Tate Poetry Prize 2020)
ISBN 978-1-912963-24-9

**Alison Dunhill.** *As Pure as Coal Dust*
(Winner of James Tate Poetry Prize 2020)
ISBN 978-1-912963-23-2

**Charles Borkhuis.** *Spontaneous Combustion*
(Winner of James Tate Poetry Prize 2021)
ISBN 978-1-912963-30-0

**Noah Falck and Matt McBride.** *Prerecorded Weather*
(Winner of James Tate Poetry Prize 2022)
ISBN 978-1-912963-39-3

**Michael Zeferino Spring.** *Kahlo's Window*
(Winner of James Tate Poetry Prize 2022)
ISBN 978-1-912963-40-9

**Dominique Hecq.** *Endgame with No Ending*
(Winner of James Tate Poetry Prize 2022)
ISBN 978-1-912963-42-3

**J V Birch.** *ice cream 'n' tar*
(Winner of James Tate Poetry Prize 2022)
ISBN 978-1-912963-43-0

**Heikki Huotari.** *To Justify the Butterfly*
(Winner of James Tate Poetry Prize 2022)
ISBN 978-1-912963-41-6

**Jeffrey Cyphers Wright.** *Fuel for Love*
(Winner of James Tate Poetry Prize 2023)
ISBN 978-1-912963-45-4

**George Kalamaras.** *That Moment of Wept*
ISBN 978-1-9995903-7-6

**George Kalamaras.** *Through the Silk-Heavy Rains*
ISBN 978-1-912963-28-7

**Anton G. Leitner.** *Selected Poems 1981–2015*
Translated from German
ISBN 978-1-9995903-8-3

Order our books from http://survisionmagazine.com

www.ingramcontent.com/pod-product-compliance
Lightning Source LLC
Chambersburg PA
CBHW071958060426
42444CB00043B/2567